MIRACLES OF THOUGHTS

RAJAT KHARE

ISBN 979-888546759-9

Contents

Preface

This book is written on the real Experiences of the Life. It contains the some effective formulas to live the True life with the definite Solutions of every unsolved Question. It is made with the Hop to help every-one or make the Life Easy and Happier.

This book is wrote in the Year 2016 on the Truths of the Life which can changes in the Human behavior or its Life to survive. And there is also transform the few thoughts according today's Environment. Now, no one can remains the old Culture, ever one have to become the Modern or Rich by the "Hook or Crook".

In this book nothing contains copy from the other Books. I am just trying to create the some-thing new and more Effect full ways to achieve the Success in the Life.

According me

*The thinking (Sense) of the Writers is same but the Wordings and Sentences are different from others.

* Every class made have the same study material, but everyone can write the exam in their wordings or styles.

* A Question is also Solve in the different ways, but the Answer is

always remains the same.

"So, change the View to change the Life."

About The Author

RAJAT KHARE

Hello, my dear Friends. I am Rajat Khare. And I live in Gwalior (M.P.). I am an International Author. This is my 2nd Book. And "Heartily Thanks to all for Appreciating my 1st Book." My hobbies are to accomplish my creative Dreams by my own Strength. I know that no valuable would be of any use, unless one recognizes their Value and Trend to perform.

Some people fall asleep quickly at night, I am not one I of them. I believe in doing every-thing with a Smile, Passions, Faith and

Delight to fulfill it.

However the tiny bag of Brain contains a source of Treasure and can offer the Accomplishments.

And I experienced that the today's Competitive World creates an unclear Decisions to face it, as like as a Child finds a precious Diamond, would be no better than a shining Stone and he would throw it away after playing with it for a short while.

"So, let's pick-up the some new Thoughts and Ideas to caught the Success and be the owner of own Destiny."

Introduction

Welcome to the Land of Thoughts.

Just as the name conveys "MIRACLES OF THOUGHT". Have this ever happened to you that, you are just strolling around or going to work, just talking to someone or watching a video and someone just strike up some words at you and that made you rethink your entire life!

As same the Book content, remark the new Ideas and Thoughts to make Boost up Life and Life-style to fulfill the Desirable Dreams.

However the tiny bag of Brain contains a source of Treasure and can offer the Accomplishments.

This read can be your everyday Dose of looking at everything from a different aspect. a

RAJAT KHARE

Wapp : 8871920419

Gmail : rajatkhare7@gmail.com

Youtube : Rajat Khare Motivationals

FB : rajatkhare123@facebook.com

FB Page : Rajat Khare - Motivationals

Insta : rajatkhared

Telegram : RajatKhare

Short - Summary

* Every Smiley face is not the happy one, some smiles are hides the lot of pain behind it.

* Emotions and Feelings can understand without a Word.

* Lover's - Will to Love, will to Chase, will to be Happy, will to never be forget, will to never be left the Hand Life Long.

* Love is the Seed, that ever grew-up from the depth of the Heart.

* Happiness is the Sweet Fruits of the Life.

* Dare the Challenges to dare the Dreams.

* Talent is ever known by the Performance.

* Bounding is only the Pre-Decided target, that's set-up by your Self.

* Great Challenges always brings the great Opportunities.

* Attraction creates the Love.

* Love ever birth in the Depth of the Heart.

* Love is the Game of Loving Hearts, Heartless people can't effort it.

* Sometimes Silence is more painful than the Noise.

* A longer relation-ship is always held on the Truth.

* Blessings and Feelings are work very quickly, but it's too effetely.

* An attachment of the Hearts birth's the wireless Connectivity between the Persons.

* Power is never be gifted, Power is ever be generate by the Long Meditation.

* Raising the Power means the rising of the Opportunities.

* Experiences are the Supporters of the Life, to create the Support in the Life.

* Potential is the Power to be the Successful Person.

* Difficulties introduce the true Caring or Faithful Persons of the Life.

* Style is the makeover of learning's in the Behavior or Nature of a Person.

* Every-one is expert in giving the Advice, but no one known's the Reality.

* Different Styles makes the Human different from others.

* Human taste can also change with the Time.

* Changing the Cloths can't change the Life, but changing the Views can change the Life.

* Human deeds deserver's the Human Result.

* Artists have the much more Creativity in side it, they need's only a chance to perform it.

* To know about the every matter is good, but every matter is not to Explore.

* Believe is the Most Powerful Source to achieve the something.

* God is only the Power to create the Positive waves.

* God never be set up the any Poundings or Limitations, it is only the Birth creation of Human minds.

* Report-cards are shows only the some Values, but not the Learning's behind it.

* Blessings and Passions are work very quietly, but it's too effetely.

* Blessings are too more effortful then the Worship.

* True Friends are the Messenger of God.

* Love increases the Love, Happiness increases the Happiness and Sadness increases the Sadness.

* Human have the Unstoppable Potential to cross the any Situations and Targets only the Will is Necessary.

* Human tiny "Bag" of the Brain contains an Eternal Treasure, which continuously use can offer the Accomplishments.

* Root of Inspiration always developed the Core of the Brain.

* Direction of thinking always guides by the Visuality that we see and also governs our behavior and Deeds.

* Attraction is only the Activeness in Manner of Thinking.

* A Life is largely shaped by the Thoughts of an Inspirational Mind.

1. CHALLENGE

1. Challenges give the Adventures in the Life.

2. Challenge is the Rope to reach the Success.

3. Challenges are awake the Human Excellence.

4. Challenges make's the Life Interesting.

5. Limits are ever built, to cross it.

6. Chase the Challenges is only the set-up of Mind to have the Progress.

7. Every Attempt gifted the Result to become the more improved.

8. Challenge can decide the Way of a Person.

9. Dare the Challenges to dare the Dreams.

10. Chase the Limit's chases the Challenges to Dare the Target.

11. Hope is the Believe to become's the Dream come True.

12. Talent is ever known by the Performance.

13. Never be give-up the Opportunities, if you have the Potential to do it.

14. Never be sad on the Mistakes, because the thousands of attempts give the thousands of new ways to have the Goal.

15. More expectations cause the more Hurt on breaking the Dream.

16. Everyone can see the Dreams in the closed Eyes, but if you can really have it then Wake-up.

17. Boundations are only the Pre-Decided target, that's set-up by your Self.

18. Great Challenges always brings the great Opportunities.

19. Beginning of the Hard-work means the beginning of the Success.

20. Challenger ever needs a chance to give up the Best. a

21. Fast-forward is good to have the Speed in the Life, but a single Inquiry is better to know about.

22. Act is ever speaking louder than the Voice.

23. Dreams are the Challenges; attempt the Challenge to have it.

24. Challenges are the Beats of the Hammer, every beat give's the Structure to the Life.

25. Every Challenge can make the Man Champion.

26. Problems are also in the Face of the Challenges to deal it.

27. Champions can never be fear to chase up the Challenges.

28. Servants are unable to take the Decisions, because they are under of the Owner Person.

29. Chance and Challenge both are the Attempt's to give the Opportunity.

30. Appreciate your Dreams to achieve and live the Dreams.

31. Challenges are the Seed of the Dream tree.

32. Beat the every Challenge that you have, one of them is the Key of the Destiny.

33. Human have the Unstoppable Potential to cross the any Situations and Targets only the Will is Necessary.

34. Never be follows the Dream, be Power the Dream can follows you.

35. It don't matter what's the People think about you, matter is that what you can thinks about yours-self.

36. Sadness is only makes the waste of Time.

37. Never be thinking too much, if you are not selected the Wrong way.

38. Give up the Best without expecting the Result.

39. Chase the Daring's of the Life, to make the Life more interesting

40. Be the Dog when you have to achieve the Opportunity.

41. Practice gives the more preferable results, then the experienced one.

42. Accept the Truth neglect the False to have a Bold Personality.

43. Every Desire is based on the Expectations.

44. Dreams are the Challenges; attempt the Challenge to have it.

45. Challenges are the Beats of the Hammer, every beat give's the Structure to the Life.

46. Every Challenge can make the Man Champion.

47. Problems are also in the Face of the Challenges to deal it.

48. Champions can never be fear to chase up the Challenges.

49. Servants are unable to take the Decisions, because they are under of the Owner Person.

50. Chance and Challenge both are the Attempt's to give the Opportunity.

51. Appreciate your Dreams to achieve and live the Dreams.

52. Challenges are the Seed of the Dream tree.

53. Beat the every Challenge that you have, one of them is the Key of the Destiny.

54. Human have the Unstoppable Potential to cross the any Situations and Targets only the Will is Necessary.

55. Never be give-up the Opportunities, if you have the Potential to do it.

56. Never be sad on the Mistakes, because the thousands of attempts give the thousands of new ways to have the Goal.

57. More expectations cause the more Hurt on breaking the Dream.

58. You have seen only the Dreams in the close Eyes, but if you really have it then Wake-up.

59. Boundations are only a Pre-Decided target, that's set-up by your Self.

60. Great Challenges always brings the great Opportunities.

61. Beginning of the Hard-work means the beginning of the Success.

62. Challenger ever needs a chance to give up the Best.

63. Fast-forward is good to have the Speed in the Life, but a single

Inquiry is better to know about.

64. Act is ever speaking louder than the Voice.

65. Never be follows the Dream, be Power the Dream can follows you.

66. It don't matter what's the People think about you, matter is that what you can thinks about yours-self.

67. Sadness is only makes the waste of Time.

68. Never be thinking too much, if you are not selected the Wrong way.

69. Give up the Best without expecting the Result.

70. Chase the Daring's of the Life, to make the Life more interesting.

71. Be the Dog when you have to achieve the Opportunity.

72. Practice gives the more preferable results, then the experienced one.

73. Accept the Truth neglect the Negative to create the Bold Personality.

74. Every Desire is based on the Expectations.

75. Dreams are the Challenges; attempt the Challenge to have it.

76. Only Challengers can face the Miracles in the Life.

77. Challengers are not ever Chase the Challenges only for the Success.

78. Challenge is the way of Thorns to have only Single Goal as a Flower at a Time.

79. Every dream comes true, when efforts become better than the Best.

80. There are only two ways to chase the Problems,
a. First Delay it for the Future.
b. Second Face it now to have a Solution.

2. HAPPINESS

01. Happiness is the Charming coin to achieve the Goal.

02. Happiness is always increases by distributing the others.

03. Happiness is ever developed the Positive Power (Thinking).

04. Happiness is the Sweet Fruits of the Life.

05. Happiness and Sadness is only the set-up of Mind.

06. God gifted the Happiness to all, so forget all the Sadness and be Happy.

07. Happiness has the Power to make the Impossible as the Possible.

08. Alive the Kid that lives in side to be the Craziness in the Life.

09. Sadness is the Valley of Death.

10. Some-times more Happiness also causes the Problem.

11. Spark of Happiness brings the Excitement in the Life to burn the Flame of Positiveness.

12. Happiness is the Seed that climb-up the Life to become its more fruitful and ever green.

13. True Happiness is ever based on the Truth.

14. Neglect those you can't like to be the more Comfort.

15. Glowing Face ever creates the Attraction.

16. Every Smiley face is not a Happy one, some smiles are hides the lot of pain behind it.

17. Some memories are too crazy that ever feels the Happiness.

18. Having the Happiness is not the great Deal, But how can you treat, it's the great Deal.

19. Love increases the Love, Happiness increases the Happiness and Sadness increases the Sadness.

20. Happiness can turn's up the Power twice.

21. Happiness and Sadness is always walking with each other as the two sides of single Coin.

22. Happiness ever attracts the Happiness.

23. If you wish to live then Kick the World to Live stay free for fulfillment the Dreams.

24. Only the Light of Happiness brings the Magical touch in the Life.

25. Some periods are the Diamond Periods of the life, these are unforgettable memories.

26. A Sweet Smile can decrease the Stress of Tensions.

27. Happiness is the greatest Achievements of the Life.

28. Small - small Happiness make's the Large.

29. The moment of the Happiness is ever feels to short as a Sweet Dream.

30. Happiness and work are the two Wheels of a Vehicle to have the Balance between Life and Work.

31. Ever be takes the Happiness and Bring out the Sadness feels you the Light.

32. A Laugh can delete all the Negative set up's in the Mind.

33. Happiness creates the Magical touch in the Life.

34. Happiness is ever seems on the Face.

35. Happiness is the Light when you put up in the Life then the Life becomes much brighter than before.

36. Happiness ever attracts the Happiness, and Sadness ever attracts the Sadness.

37. Sad moments are ever be Freeze for the Long times in the Mind.

38. Beauty is never being end; it always remains in the Heart.

39. Without the Mixture Gold is also not becomes the Pure.

40. God is ever favoring to those, who are ever Worship the Work.

41. Celebration is also the Source of the Power and the Happiness.

42. Happiness is lies at the every Step of the Life you have to only pick it up.

43. Golden memories are ever the best Memories to be the Happy.

44. Some Pranks are converting into the Happiest moments of the Life.

45. Stay with the Happiness is not the big deal, if you want too.

46. Happiness and Sadness are the two sides of the Single Coin.

47. Having the Fun is not meaning the absence of the Sincearness.

48. Happiness increases the Possibility of Success.

49. Happiness makes the Life more Delightful.

50. A Touch of Happiness creates the Power to make the whole World too Beautiful.

51. Angerness burn up the large Quantity of Blood.

52. If you wish then you smell the Happiness, feel the Pleasure, and have the Excitement in the Life.

53. Fun is the moment when the Happiness and the Human can inter-face with each other.

54. If you wish to live then Kick the World to Live stay free for fulfillment the Dreams.

55. Only the Light of Happiness brings the Magical touch in the Life.

56. Some periods are the Diamond Periods of the life, these are unforgettable memories.

57. A Sweet Smile can decrease the Stress of Tensions.

58. Happiness is the greatest Achievements of the Life.

59. Small - small Happiness make's the Large.

60. The moment of the Happiness is ever feels to short as a Sweet Dream.

61. Happiness and work are the two Wheels of a Vehicle to have the Balance between Life and Work.

62. Ever be takes the Happiness and Bring out the Sadness feels you the Light.

63. A Laugh can delete all the Negative set up's in the Mind.

64. Happiness is the Seed that climb-up the Life to become its more fruitful and ever green.

65. True Happiness is ever based on the Truth.

66. Neglect those you can't like to be the more Comfort.

67. Glowing Face ever creates the Attraction.

68. Every Smiley face is not the Happy one, some smiles are hides the lot of pain behind it.

69. Some memories are too crazy that ever feels the Happiness.

70. Having the Happiness is not the great Deal, But how can you treat, it's the great Deal.

71. Love increases the Love, Happiness increases the Happiness and Sadness increases the Sadness.

72. Happiness can turn's up the Power twice.

73. Happiness and Sadness is always walking with each other as the two sides of single Coin.

74. Happiness creates the Magical touch in the Life.

75. Happiness is ever seems on the Face.

76. Happiness is the Light when you put up in the Life then the Life becomes much brighter than before.

77. Happiness ever attracts the Happiness, and Sadness ever attracts the Sadness.

78. Sad moments are ever be Freeze for the Long times in the Mind.

79. Beauty is never being end; it always remains in the Heart.

80. Without the Mixture Gold is also not becomes the Pure.

81. God is ever favoring to those, who are ever Worship the Work.

82. Celebration is also the Source of the Power and the Happiness.

83. Happiness is lies at the every step of the Life you have to only pick it up.

3. LOVE

01. Love is the Virus that flows in the Heart and Damage all the sets-ups of the Mind.

02. Love is the Opportunity, to having the Peace-full part of the World.

03. Love is the Sense of the Human, which makes them Nonsense.

04. Love is the Challenge, to chase the Happiness.

05. Attraction creates the Love.

06. Love is the efforts between the Hearts.

07. Love has no Language; it knows only the Language of Love.

08. Love conations no Color, no Religion, it have only the Love and Peace.

09. Love ever birth in the Depth of the Heart.

10. Love is the Game of Loving Hearts, Heartless people can't effort it.

11. Sometimes Silence is more painful than the Noise.

12. Attraction is the first stage of Love.

13. Love is the Spark, that burn's the Thousand's of flame in the single Time into the Heart.

14. Love is the Gift of God to being Happy, in what you have.

15. Love is the Creation of God to fly over the Dream views.

16. Love is the stock of Emotions.

17. Love is ever set up in the Heart, without the using of Brain.

18. Lover's - Will to Love, will to Chase, will to be Happy, will to never be forget, will to never be left the Hand Life Long.

19. A longer relation-ship is always held on the Truth.

20. Love is the Flame that's ever being burning into the Heart.

21. As much you can distribute the Love as much it can increases more and more.

22. Blessings and Feelings are work very quietly, but it's too perfectly.

23. Emotions and Feelings can understand without a Word.

24. Love is the Seed, that ever grew-up from the depth of the Heart.

25. Broken Heart hardly trusted on the other.

26. In the Love Expressions can says everything without a Word.

27. An attachment of the Hearts birth's the wireless Connectivity between the Persons.

28. In the Love Feelings are more easily to understand then the Words.

29. Love is the Blind bird that flies over the Peace and Happiness in the Hearts.

30. Every beautiful thing is not as beautiful as it looks like.

31. Peace and Love is the solution of any Problem, but ever keeps the second option as the Strength.

32. Love increases the Love, Happiness increases the Happiness and Sadness increases the Sadness.

33. Beauty is ever remains in the Heart not on the Face.

34. Broken Heart has the much better experience to Select or achieve the best.

35. Heart is the Sensitive Part of the Body, which is break or hurt very effectively.

36. True friends are never being demand but adjust in that you have.

37. Heart is the House of Love; Happiness is ever remains' in it as the Golden Memories.

38. An Animal is much more Royal in the Relations.

39. Friends are ever as like as the Rose, Who ever brings the smile on the Face, create the Fragrances in the Life to makes it more Sweeter.

40. In Love it doesn't matter what you are and what you have to Achieve.

41. Those who slipped on the Beauty those are the Temporary Attraction.

42. Love have the Power to bring down the hole World into the Legs.

43. No one can Creates the Love, no one can Destroys the Love, and Love is the Blessings of God.

44.How much Happiness is given by the Love as much more Sadness is given by the Love on breaking it.

45. Love is not effort by the Heartless People.

46. The moment with the Loving ones is ever feels to short as a Sweet Dream.

47. Every Relation-ship creates it's on Chemistry.

48. Love is the Game of the Passion.

49. Appreciate the Desires to have the Wings.

50. To create the Relation-ship is too easy, but to leave it, it's too difficult.

51. Relationship is the Single thread of many faces.

52. Logic is not necessary in the Love; there is only the Feelings that's inter-connected the each other.

53. Eyes never be flow the Tears, it's only the Emotions of the Heart that flow into the Eyes.

54. The Deepness of the Love is so deep, that no one can measure it.

55. Love is the Track of Blindness.

56. Love becomes the Human as the without break Vehicle.

57. Well Behave Person is ever Close to the Heart.

58. To have the Position in the some one's heart is not too easy.

59. More Lovers' of the single Person at the single time ever because the harmful to the Person.

60. More Love is ever be the Harmful.

61. Love is ever glowing on the Face.

62. Love is the Single thread of two faces.

63. Believe is the Root of Strong Relation-Ship.

64. True Love means the connection between the Hearts, Feelings, Emotions and the Happiness.

65. Love can take the Human at the High.

66. Love is only the superb Understanding between the Persons.

67. Sweet Persons ever meet the Sweet Personality.

68. The Attachment of the Heart is the connection of two Souls.

69. More Emotions can cerates the Confusions.

70. Heart is the Tree of Love, which have several of Sweet Fruits, Branches of Love and Beauty of the Flowers.

71. Seed of Love needs only the Caring to grow up.

72. Lover's can lose the six Senses and makes them Nonsense.

73. Happiness is ever be celebrated in the Groups, because no one can celebrate the Life alone.

74. Love can easily understand and cerate's the Passions in the People.

75. Soft voice is ever be creates the Attraction.

76. Heat is the set up box of the Sentiments, which flows the Sentiments in the Person.

77. Relations are not based on the Blood sometimes connectivity of the Heart is more than the Blood Relations.

78. Love is the very dangerous illness, it contains only to options. They are – Do or Die.

79. A Crunch of the Love makes the Life more Cruncher.

80. Love ever reduce the Distance between the People and tied them into a new Relation.

81. Love is never be Create by the Medicine and it never be Killed by the Poison.

82. Love is ever increases on the Spending.

83. Love is the Gate-Way of the Heaven.

84. Love can create the Magical touch in the Life.

85. Lovers can ever design its World, they never be mind the other

World.

86. Love is the Sense of Attachments of the Hearts to create the World as the Desire.

87. Illness is ever be cure by the Treatment, but the broken Heart is never be cure by the any Treatment.

88. In love every moment is feeling as the Pleasure of the Life.

89. Love makes the Person mindless, and then every Decision is ever taken by the Heart.

90. Love is automatically teach, how to ignore the World, to have the Comfort.

91. Love is the unique creation of the God.

92. Love is the Crunch of Happiness, with the multiple layers of Feelings and Emotions.

93. Love is not the Efforts of Single Side, it moves when the Efforts of both sides are equally worked.

94. Attraction between the Persons causes the format of the Love.

95. Attraction between the Hearts creates the Reflection of Love.

96. Love is like the Insect which can catch the one time then it never be leaves.

97. Emotions can understand the Feelings without a Word.

98. Love is the Seed, that ever grew-up from the depth of the Heart.

99. Broken Heart hardly trusted on the other.

100. In the Love Expressions can says everything without a Word.

101. An attachment of the Hearts birth's the wireless Connectivity between the Persons.

102. In the Love Feelings are more easily to understand then the Words.

103. Love is the Blind bird that flies over the Peace and Happiness in the Hearts.

104. Every beautiful thing is not as beautiful as it looks.

105. Peace and Love is the solution of any Problem, but ever keeps the second option as the Strength.

106. Love increases the Love, Happiness increases the Happiness and Sadness increases the Sadness.

107. Love have the Power to bring down the hole World into the Legs.

108. No one can Creates the Love, no one can Destroys the Love, and Love is the Blessings of God.

109. How much Happiness is given by the Love as much more Sadness is given by the Love on breaking it.

110. Love is not effort by the Heartless People.

111. The moment with the Loving ones is ever feels to short as a Sweet Dream.

112. Every Relation-ship creates it's on Chemistry.

113. Love is the Game of the Passion.

114. Appreciate the Desires to have the Wings.

115. To create the Relation-ship is too easy, but to leave it, it's too difficult.

116. Relationship is the Single thread of many faces.

117. Logic is not necessary in the Love; there is only Feelings those are inter-connected the Attachment of Relations.

118. Eyes never be flow the Tears, it's only the Emotions of the Heart that flow into the Eyes.

119. The Deepness of the Love is so deep, that no one can measure it.

120. Love is the Track of Blindness.

121. Love becomes the Human as the without break Vehicle.

122. Well Behave Person is ever Close to the Heart.

123. To have the Position in the some one's heart is not too easy.

124. More Lovers' of the single Person at the single time ever because the harmful to the Person.

125. More Love is ever being the Harmful.

126. Love is ever glowing on the Face.

127. Love is the Single thread of two faces.

128. Believe is the Root of Strong Relation-Ship.

129. Lover's - Will to Love, will to Chase, will to be Happy, will to never be forget, will to never be left the Hand Life Long.

130. Words + Feelings give the much better Response.

131. A Happy life is ever be Shaped by the - Feel + Act + Emotions = Great Happiness.

4. Power

01. Power is the Strength that chases the World.

02. Limits are ever tag to Break-up it.

03. Will-Power is the biggest source of the Success.

04. Power never chooses the Direction; it is chosen by the Owner.

05. More Power ever makes the Man Cruel.

06. Power is the Source to Success.

07. Never be Fear, if you can't do the anything wrong.

08. Craziness is the Power that crosses all the Difficulties easily in the Fun.

09. Power ever set up the Goals to Achieve.

10. Power is never be gifted, Power is ever be generate by the Long Meditation.

11. Will-Power is the Gate-way to create the Desirable world.

12. Alive the Kid that lives in side to be the Craziness about the Work.

13. Never be run behind the Future, try to be run forward in the Present.

14. Power is the Spark, who's able to burn the whole World.

15. Raising the Power means the rising of the Opportunities.

16. Hard-worker and Responsible Person are ever be in the Stress, but the Enjoyable Person is ever be work the Fun.

17. Experiences are the Supporters of the Life, to create the Support in the Life.

18. Potential is the Power to be the Successful Person.

19. Never be break down yourself, create the some changes to have the more better result.

20. Difficulties introduce the true Caring or Faithful Persons of the Life.

21. Attitude is the first impression of the Human.

22. Rising of Confidence means the Rising of the Power.

23. Risk creates the Position of do or die.

24. In the depth of Darkness a single ray of hope increases the Power Two-times more.

25. Negative vibrations ever birth the Negativity.

26. Every decision is not the Correct one, so always be have the Back-up Plans.

27. Boldness in the Voice indicates the Confidence in the Person.

28. In the Sorrow a single point of Happiness brings up the Potential to Live.

29. Attempt is vibrant better, then the Chance.

30. Hidden Potential ever comes out, when the Thinking becomes the Bold.

31. Appreciate an Increase the Confidence.

32. Revenge ever births the Evil in the Human.

33. Without having the Wings Talent (Power) is nothing.

34. Life can teaches us more than the Expectations.

35. Every Talent got the Stage after the Long Meditation.

36. Talent ever wants only the Opportunity.

37. Do something is better than the Do nothing.

38. More expectations can fall the Man more badly.

39. Crowd is ever be runs in the Direction of Flow.

40. Perfection is ever be caused by the Long Meditation on it.

41. Never be follows the Dream, be Power the Dream can follows you.

42. Having the Support creates the great Potential towards the Target.

43. Chair up ever increases the Capability to achieve the Goal.

44. Calibration is also the Source of the Power and the Happiness.

45. Power is only the Strength that you have.

46. Show off is not the Weapon for ever, because it's only the Artificial Curtain.

47. Rocking person ever be Rock's the Personality.

48. Feel the Power to have the Power.

49. Defeat is never being mean to loss the Dignity.

50. A seed (Starting) of Power grow up into the big Tree.

51. Thinking can never be change the Events, but the Event can change the Thinking.

52. Crowd is never representing the Unity; Unity is always represented by the Connected People.

53. Angriness never chases the Goal.

54. Convert your energy as the Power to have the Power.

55. In the depth of Darkness a single ray of hope increases the Power Two-times more.

56. Negative vibrations ever birth the Negativity.

57. Every decision is not the Correct one, so always be have the Back-up Plans.

58. Boldness in the Voice indicates the Confidence in the Person.

59. In the Sorrow a single point of Happiness brings up the Potential to Live.

60. Attempt is vibrant better, then the Chance.

61. Hidden Potential ever comes out, when the Thinking becomes the Bold.

62. Appreciate an Increase the Confidence.

63. Revenge ever births the Evil in the Human.

64. Without having the Wings Talent (Power) is nothing.

65. Life can teaches us more than the Expectations.

66. Never be run behind the Future, try to be run forward in the Present.

67.Power is the Spark, who's able to burn the whole World.

68. Raising the Power means the rising of the Opportunities.

69. Hard-worker and Responsible Person are ever be in the Stress, but the Enjoyable Person is ever be work the Fun.

70. Experiences are the Supporters of the Life, to create the Support in the Life.

71. Potential is the Power to be the Successful Person.

72. Never be break down yourself, create the some changes to have the more better result.

73. Difficulties introduce the true Caring or Faithful Persons of the Life.

74. Attitude is the first impression of the Human.

75. Rising of Confidence means the Rising of the Power.

76. Risk creates the Position of do or die.

77. Every Talent got the Stage after the Long Meditation.

78. Talent ever wants only the Opportunity.

79. Do something is better than the Do nothing.

80. More expectations can fall the Man more badly.

67. Crowd is ever being runs in the Direction of Flow.

82. Perfection is ever be caused by the Long Meditation on it.

83. Never be follows the Dream, be Power the Dream can follows you.

84. Having the Support creates the great Potential towards the Target.

85. Chair up ever increases the Capability to achieve the Goal.

86. Calibration is also the Source of the Power and the Happiness.

87. Power is only the Strength that you have.

88. Show off is not the Weapon for ever, because it's only the Artificial Curtain.

5. STYLE

01. Style is the makeover of learning's in the Behavior or Nature of a Person.

02. Human Style and Behavior decides the Human Destiny.

03. Human Style can analyses their Personality.

04. Style never be select the Human, Human can select the Style as it Behavior.

05. Look's and Style are the make-ups of Human Position.

06. Every-one is expert in giving the Advice, but no one knew the Reality.

07. Different Styles makes the Human different from others.

08. Human taste can also change with the Time.

09. Style is always set up in the Behavior no one can change it.

10. Style is ever be gifted as the Environment, that you have.

11. Cloths are the Curtains that hide the Actuality behind it.

12. Change the Style to change the Life.

13. Target is never be achieved by the Thinking.

14. Everyone have to Design it's on Style.

15. More meeting cause decreases the Value of the Person.

16. Everyone have to maintain its image on its self.

17. Changing the Cloths can't change the Life, but changing the Views can change the Life.

18. Blinking represents the Presence, as the Up and Down in the Life.

19. A human deed deserves the Human Result.

20. No work did on the full Truth; it is also seeing in the Holy Books.

21. Artists have the much more Creativity in side it, they need's only a chance to perform it.

22. Having the Passion means to have the Potential.

23. Respect ever makes the Reputation.

24. Passion creates the Steps towards the Success.

25. To know about the every matter is good, but every matter is not to Explore.

26. Avoiding is not the Permanent solution of any Work.

27. A chance is the Golden Opportunity never leave it.

28. Boldness ever decreases the Confidence of the Front one.

29. Meet and Drop is also the Part of the Life towards the Progress.

30. Craziness about the Work, turn's on the Night as the Day.

31. Aloneness is the biggest Source of Depression.

32. Failure is nothing it's only the Chance that you Lost.

33. Ever do that that you have to Wish, for achieving that that you have to Dream.

34. To Complete the Work is not so important, but at which level you keep your work it's the Importance.

35. An unnecessary thought makes the Person heavy or Disturbed nothing more then it.

36. Sometimes little fun creates the big Problem.

37. Artists are not the God, but they have the Creativity to Direct the Life.

38. Strategies are only give the Shape to the Future, if the Present base is remains to Build.

39. Potential is never be calculated by the Nature.

40. To achieve the Thing is not the Potential, but how to use it, it's the potential.

41. Problems can make the Man Stronger.

42. Incomplete Information is the more Harmful then the without Information.

43. Attitude describes the Personality of the Person.

44. Point out the Positiveness of others to apply in the Life.

45. Chill up the Mode of the Life to have the chillness in the Life.

46. Distribute the Happiness to have the Happiness.

47. Popularity is ever increases the Demand.

48. Sometimes have the Privacy is not the Wrong decision.

49. Efforts can convert the Time and Situations as your comfort.

50. Creativity makes the Life creative with the Amazing touch.

51. Violent nature can destroy the Whole World.

52. Sleeping is the best Treatment to overcome the Stress.

53. Never be fall the Tears, ever be keep it as the Power and applies on the Target to dare it.

54. Zoom your creations to zoom the World.

55. Home Size is always comparing to the Heart.

56. Big rulers are never be have the time to check out the Small-

small Problems.

57. Always Keep the Trump in the Hand, to turn up the Game.

58. Build the Weakness as the Potential to chase the World more effect fully.

59. Power is never be denoted by the Size and Shape.

60. Passion creates the Steps towards the Success.

61. To know about the every matter is good, but every matter is not to Explore.

62. Avoiding is not the Permanent solution of any Work.

63. A chance is the Golden Opportunity never leaves it.

64. Boldness ever decreases the Confidence of the Front one.

65. Meet and Drop is also the Part of the Life towards the Progress.

66. Craziness about the Work, turn's on the Night as the Day.

67. Aloneness is the biggest Source of Depression.

68. Failure is nothing it's only the Chance that you Lost.

69. Ever do that that you have to Wish, for Achieving that that you have to Dream.

70. To Complete the Work is not so important, but at which level you keep your work it's the Importance.

71. Target is never be achieved by the Thinking.

72. Everyone have to Design it's on Style.

73. More meeting cause decreases the Value of the Person.

74. Everyone have to maintain its image on its self.

75. Changing the Cloths can't change the Life, but changing the Views can change the Life.

76. Blinking represents the Presence, as the Up and Down in the Life.

77. A human deed deserves the Human Result.

78. No work did on the full Truth; it is also seeing in the Holy Books.

79. Artists have the much more Creativity in side it, they need's only a chance to perform it.

80. Having the Passion means to have the Potential.

81. Respect ever makes the Reputation.

82. Passion creates the Steps towards the Success.

83. To know about the every matter is good, but every matter is not to Explore.

84. Avoiding is not the Permanent solution of any Work.

85. A chance is the Golden Opportunity never be leave it.

86. Boldness ever decreases the Confidence of the Front one.

87. Meet and Drop is also the Part of the Life towards the Progress.

88. Craziness about the Work, turn's on the Night as the Day.

89. Aloneness is the biggest Source of Depression.

90. Failure is nothing it's only a Chance that you Lost.

91. Ever do that that you have to Wish, for Achieving that that you have to Dream.

92. To Complete the Work is not so important, but at which level you keep your work it's the Importance.

6. BELIEF

1. Blessings are the Source of the Flam that burning in the Heart.

2. God is only the Believe to be the Confident.

3. God is the Powerful source to have the Power.

4. Believe is the Most Powerful Source to achieve the something.

5. Blessing's ever producing the Power that you needed.

6.Blessing ever produces the Positive Energy.

7. Good will, work ever give's the Happiness, Positiveness.

8. God is only the Power to create the Positive waves.

9.God never be set up the any Boundations or Limitations, it is only the Birth creation of Human minds.

10. God gifted the Believe to the Human, to do the practice on the Believe to have the Target.

11. Report-cards are shows only the some Values, but not the

Learning's behind it.

12. God is only the Believe Power of the People.

13. Crisis's the moment to serve the Difficulties for a Period.

14. Blessings and Passions are work very Quietly, but it's too perfectly.

15. Blessings are too more effortful then the Worship.

16. True Friends are the Messenger of God.

17. Give up others is the great Strength, but sometimes it causes the big Mistake.

18. A Good deed is more Powerful then the God Worship.

19. Efforts can Vibrant the Blessings to achieve the Target.

20. Hope and Deed never be left the Hand of the Human.

21. Lightness and Darkness are the two sides of single Coin.

22. Dream is the Painting, Paint your Dreams.

23. Miracle are ever cause by the Good Deeds.

24. Meditation creates the power to have the Attention.

25. Fear is only the Set up of Mind.

26. Cleaning is the work of Thief and Sweeper, but the Thief provides the Sorrow, and the Sweeper provides the Peace of Heart.

27. Profit or Loss is the two Faces of the Single coin.

28. Where there is the Profit, there is also having the Loss.

29. Expensive things have the Qualities to have the Expensive.

30. Having the Quality, not mean by having the Potential.

31. Miracles are ever cause by the Efforts.

32. Feel to be Proud ever one are the Child of God, and everyone have the Some Different Potential to Rule over the World

33. Positive waves creates the Positive Power, ever be flow the Waves in the Heart to be the Positive.

34. Never be tell a Lie, but never be tell the fully Truth to everyone.

35. Blind believe is as the Friendship with the close Eyes.

36. Helpful People are ever being full of Potentials as the loaded Tree of the Fruits.

37. Fear is only the Seed of the Mind.

38. Helping others gives the Pleasure in the Life.

39. A Laugh can burn's all the Sadness of the Human.

40. God is only the Believe Power of the People.

41. Crisis's the moment to serve the Difficulties for a Period.

42. Blessings and Passions are work very Quietly, but it's too perfectly.

43. Blessings are too more effortful then the Worship.

44. True Friends are the Messenger of God.

45. Give up others is the great Strength, but sometimes it causes the big Mistake.

46. A Good deed is more Powerful then the God Worship.

47. Efforts can Vibrant the Blessings to achieve the Target.

48. Hope and Deed never be left the Hand of the Human.

49. Lightness and Darkness are the two sides of single Coin.

50. Dream is the Painting, Paint your Dreams.

51. Miracle are ever cause by the Good Deeds.

52. Meditation creates the power to have the Attention.

53. Fear is only the Set up of Mind.

54. Cleaning is the work of Thief and Sweeper, but the Thief provides the Sorrow, and the Sweeper provides the Peace of Heart.

55. Profit or Loss is the two Faces of the Single coin.

56. Where there is the Profit, there is also having the Loss.

57. Expensive things have the Qualities to have the Expensive.

58. Having the Quality, not mean by having the Potential.

59. Miracles are ever cause by the Efforts.

60. Feel to be Proud ever one are the Child of God, and everyone have the Some Different Potential to Rule over the World

61. Positive waves creates the Positive Power, ever be flow the Waves in the Heart to be the Positive.

62. Never be tell a Lie, but never be tell the fully Truth to everyone.

63. Blind believe is as the Friendship with the close Eyes.

64. Blessings are the Source of the Flam that burning in the Heart.

65. God is only the Believe to be the Confident.

66. God is the Powerful source to have the Power.

67. Believe is the Most Powerful Source to achieve the something.

68. Blessing's ever producing the Power that you needed.

69. Blessing ever produces the Positive Energy.

70. Good will, work ever give's the Happiness, Positiveness.

71. God is only the Power to create the Positive waves.

72. God never be set up the any Boundations or Limitations, it is only the Birth creation of Human minds.

73. God gifted the Believe to the Human, to do the practice on the Believe to have the Target.

74. Report-cards are shows only the some Values, but not the Learning's behind it.

7. VISION

01. Vision is only the view to see the Achievements.

02. Vision contains the Versions to choose or see the single View.

03. The Visions have the power to make the Success (Happiness) or Defeat (Sadness) in the Human.

04. Vision birth the Views to see the Moments in Positive otherwise in Negative views.

05. Single Vision always has the Single Destination.

06. Vision is only the sight to see the Views as you want to take it.

07. Vision is also the Power in its self.

08. Fairness is always lies on the Liar's face.

09. Vision set up is always denotes your thinking or the gap between you and the Goal.

10. Vision ever gifted the Potential to have the Positive side of happiness.

11. Every incident is important, if you take it in the correct Manner.

12. Believe is the Vision to achieve the Goal.

13. Sadness is comes in the every one's Life, but it's your wish to spend it in the Sorrow or Happiness.

14. Changing the Cloths can't the Life, but changing the Views can change the Life.

15. Make the Talent as the Power, Skill as the Weapons, and Dream as the Vision to achieve as the Best.

16. Broken human can't take the right Decisions, because of the Depression.

17. Every helping Person is not the Friend, ever check out them.

18. Did the Mistake is not the Fault, but if you can't correct it, after knowing the Mistake that's the Fault.

19. Never be sad on the Defeat, because every big Inventers reaches there Place after the having thousand's of Mistakes.

20. Realization is the biggest Punishment to the Doer.

21. Aloneness increases the Human Talents.

22. How much Problems you can solve in the Present, as much less Problems you have to solve in the Future.

23. Pain is lies in the every one's Life, but some are showing it or others are hiding it.

24. To create the Problem is too easy, but to solve the Problem is too Difficult.

25. No one focus what you are, every one focus on what's you have become.

26. Planning's are not ever be the Successful, because of the Conditions of Time.

27. Never be belongs on any one, because no one known's the Actual Condition.

28. Dreams are ever be created by the Potential or Qualities of a Person.

29. Every Environment gives the same Qualities that are automatically copied in the Hunan Nature.

30. Sadness is the Poison that can kill the Costiveness.

31. Defeat is also necessary to know the Actual Position.

32. Fear is only the Approach of the Mind.

33. Result is ever being showing that you Gained.

34. Every one's desire to open the Wings, to have the freeness.

35. Human approach can make it up and Down.

36. Small-small mistakes transform the Crises.

37. A Laugh can refresh the Human with the Positivity.

38. Craziness strikes the moments of Happiness.

39. Wings are not ever needed to fly; only the Will is necessary.

40. Luck is ever favors' the Daring Person.

41. Golden ways ever have the Golden Opportunities.

42. Sadness is the Virus that can affect all over the Mind set up's.

43. Never be fear, if you can't do anything Wrong.

44. To calculate the Profit is easy, but to calculate the Loss is too difficult.

45. Only the Tired Person knows the value of Rest.

46. Every Dimension creates the Different vision in the Mind.

47. Team work makes the Work as the way of Happiness to Achieve the Target.

48. Dignity ever creates the Position in the Flock of the People.

49. Very few know the Truth, but everyone use their advices to be the Greater.

50. Basic information is never being created; it is always copied from the Source.

51. Thoughts are the Seed of the Mind.

52. Multitalented People always have the multiple of works to do.

53. Golden memories are the Soul of the Life.

54. Every one focused on the Work, no one wants' to know, what you are?

55. An Approach can change the Human.

56. Discard changes creates the great Impact on the Life style.

57. Dreams are the Portable vision to chase the Target.

58. Exchanging of views gives the New and effect full Ways to Achieve the Success.

59. Human behavior is ever express that what he has gained in the Life.

60. People wants to know only open their mouth, when they are Right or wrong.

61. Realization is the biggest Punishment to the Doer.

62. Aloneness increases the Human Talents.

63. How much Problems you can solve in the Present, as much less Problems you have to solve in the Future.

64. Pain is lies in the every one's Life, but some are showing it or others are hiding it.

65. To create the Problem is too easy, but to solve the Problem is too difficult.

66. No one focus what you are, every one focus on what's you have become.

67. Planning's are not ever be the Successful, because of the Conditions of Time.

68. Never be belongs on any one, because no one known's the Actual Condition.

69. Dreams are ever be created by the Potential or Qualities of a Person.

70. Every Environment gives the same Qualities that are automatically copied in the Hunan Nature.

71. Every incident is important, if you take it in the correct Manner.

72. Believe is the Vision to achieve the Goal.

73. Sadness is comes in the every one's Life, but it's your wish to spend it in the Sorrow or Happiness.

74. Changing the Cloths can't the Life, but changing the Views can change the Life.

75. Make the Talent as the Power, Skill as the Weapons, and Dream as the Vision to achieve as the Best.

76. Broken human can't take the right Decisions, because of the Depression.

77. Every helping Person is not the Friend, ever check out them.

78. Did the Mistake is not the Fault, but if you can't correct it, after knowing the Mistake that's the Fault.

79. Never be sad on the Defeat, because every big Inventers reaches there Place after the having thousand's of Mistakes.

8. DESTINY

01. Destiny is only the Concept that resulted in the favor on the Nature of time.

02. Destiny never be gives the any Solution without applying the any efforts.

03. Destiny only gives the way to move on.

04. Destiny never be final the Result's, it's only give the Way to Walk.

05. Believe is the biggest Source to Design the Destiny.

06. Destiny never be set up the Past, Present and Future.

07. Destiny ever gifted the way, to reach to the Success.

08. In the Darkness, Shadow is also leave's the Hand of a Person.

09. Destiny is never being written before the Act.

10. Destiny never be declare the Future, it is ever created as the Act is given in the Present.

11. No one can make's the Destiny and no one can destroyed it, it's only you to give the Way.

12. A believe can make's the Destiny.

13. Destiny never make's the Way; it's only give that you have to Deserve.

14. Desires are converting into the Destiny.

15. Destiny ever be gives the Opportunities' to Attempt it.

16. Everyone have to Design it's on Destiny.

17. Great Destiny is the great Designing's of the great Deservers.

18. You are the Writer, you are the Director and you are the Actor, then what's waiting for go and bring out the Talent.

19. In the Difficulty every-one turning their faces, when needed as help.

20. Passions always Deserves more than the Destiny.

21. There is no security in the Life, so be the Happy and brings the Happiness.

22. Great Intension ever brings up the great Opportunity.

23. Destiny gives the Path to walk, but how it is depend on you.

24. Appearing moments are not ever be the same as it looks like.

25. Strength is always having the chance to show the Potential, never be waiting for the Chance.

26. Courage can turn's up the Destiny in the Favor.

27. No one see the Past, People believe on the Present what you are.

28. Past can never be Shape up the Future.

29. Destiny is the wet Mud; give the Structure to the Life.

30. Human have to face the Problems there is no other way.

31. Craziness is the totally madness to have that you want at any Way.

32. Destiny is only give the Wings, but how to fly it's your Matter.

33. Chance and Chair never be Stay Blank.

34. Goods work increases the Expectations.

35. Life never be demand's you the nothing, then why you are demanding so.

36. Destiny never be fulfill the requirements, it needs only the Hard work.

37. Chance and Chair never be waiting for the Longer.

38. Sometimes Condition is not in the Favor, which makes the critical Position to choose that you can't like.

39. Blind walkers are ever walking on the way of Destiny, but never be effort to change the Destiny.

40. Target achievers never be run behind the Target, but they ever try to give the Best.

41. Human are never be choose the Way, it is ever be choose by the Destiny.

42. Human soul is ever knows that what's the Wrong and Right, but the Mind is only knows the Profit or Loss.

43. A believe can make's the Destiny.

44. Destiny never be make's the way, it's only give that you have to Deserve.

45. Desires are converting into the Destiny.

46. Destiny ever be gives the Opportunities' to Attempt it.

47. Everyone have to Design it's on Destiny.

48. Great Destiny is the great Designing's of the great Deservers.

49. You are the Writer, you are the Director and you are the Actor, then what's waiting for go and bring out the Talent.

50. In the Difficulty every-one turning their faces, when needed as help.

51.Passions always Deserves more than the Destiny.

52. There is no security in the Life, so be the Happy and brings the Happiness.

53. Great Intension ever brings up the great Destiny.

54. Goods work increases the Expectations.

55. Life never be demand's you the nothing, then why you are demanding so.

56. Destiny never be fulfill the requirements, it needs only the Hard work.

57. Chance and Chair never be waiting for the Longer.

58. Sometimes Condition is not in the Favor, which makes the critical Position to choose that you can't like.

59. Blind walkers are ever walking on the way of Destiny, but never be effort to change the Destiny.

60. Target achievers never be run behind the Target, but they ever try to give the Best.

61. Human are never be choose the Way, it is ever be choose by the Destiny.

62. Human soul is ever knows that what's the Wrong and Right, but the Mind is only knows the Profit or Loss.

63. A believe can make's the Destiny.

64. Destiny is ever be mention by the Thinking + Hard Work.

65. Work over the Present = Work over the Future over the Destiny.

66. When the Self believe reaches at a highest point, then the whole Universe become the Companion for us to fulfill our Believes.

67. Every Thing is looking like a so Bigger till you can't able to Reach or Afford it.

68. Map your Life, to Map up your Destination as your Destiny.

9. SUCCESS

01. Success is only mean by the fulfillment of Dreams.

02. Success always need's the Passions.

03. Dare the Challenges to dare the Success.

04. Success is only the source of Thinking to have it.

05. Be the Power, Power is ever chase the Success.

06. Success is only the Vision to Have it.

07. Never be wait for the right Time or Destiny, do that, that's in your Hand.

08. Craze is the short period Power, but it gives the very effectual Results.

09. Success is ever set up by the Hard- Worker.

10. Talent is ever known by its Performance.

11. Will-Power is the Gate-way to achieve the Success.

12. Hope is the Root of any Success.

13. Passions cause the rises towards the Success.

14. Ignoration is the first step to be the Defeated.

15. Desires are the Wings to reach the High, touch the Sky.

16. Back-up plan is the Back Bone of the Success.

17. Having the Believe is the Source of the Success.

18. Negativeness leads the human to the Defeat.

19. Positiveness is not the Intension; Positiveness is the Power that flow's in the Blood.

20. Only the Hope holds the Hand to the Success.

21. A Happy life contains the long Hard-work behind it.

22. An Animal can teaches the much more batter then the Human.

23. Heart, Soul, and Body together combine to make's the Perfect Person.

24. Advantage and Disadvantage is always walking with each other as the Light and Shadow.

25. Dare the Fault, to make it correct.

26. Short and Easy ways are ever be the Fake and Dump Ways.

27. The efforts to become's the Better is the Sprit to break the gate way of Success.

28. Boldness in the Voice makes the Lion as the King of the Jungle.

29. Drag and Drop is the Nature of the Environment.

30. Crack all of the Limitations and Boundations that tries' to make's you the Stop to reaching the Target.

31. Only the Light of Happiness brings the Magical touch in the Life.

32. Wings are always open to touch the sky.

33. Past is the Story, Present is the Realty and Future is the Dream.

34. Open the wings to reach the High.

35. Blind Strikers are very hardly Achieve the Success.

36. Every intension has the Purpose towards the Success.

37. Efforts are the Pillar of the Success.

38. Courage becomes the Ladder to the Success.

39. Charming Works are much more difficult than the Labor works.

40. Success is never be known's the Language, it's only known's the Hard Work.

41. A Performance makes the Ten-times better then the before.

42. Angriness is the First evil towards the Success.

43. No one can understand you, much better than your -self.

44. No one can solve your problem; you have to understand it on your-Self.

45. Never be taking any step without the Permission of the Mind and Heart.

46. Happiness increases the Possibility of Success.

47. Everyone have the ride to See the Dreams, but who works hard to complete it, they are the True Viewers.

48. Short and Easy ways are ever be the Fake and Dump Ways.

49. The efforts to become's the Better is the Sprit to break the gate way of Success.

50. Boldness in the Voice makes the Lion as the King of the Jungle.

51. Drag and Drop is the Nature of the Environment.

52. Crack all of the Limitations and Boundations that tries to make's you the Stop to reaching the Target.

53. Only the Light of Happiness brings the Magical touch in the Life.

54. Wings are always open to touch the sky.

55. Past is the Story, Present is the Realty and Future is the Dream.

56. Open the wings to reach the High.

57. Blind Strikers are very hardly Achieve the Success.

58. Every intension has the Purpose towards the Success.

59. Ignorant is the first step to be the Defeated.

60. Desires are the Wings to reach the High, touch the Sky.

61. Back-up plan is the Back Bone of the Success.

62. Having the Believe is the Source of the Success.

63. Negativeness leads the human to the Defeat.

64. Positiveness is not the Intension; Positiveness is the Power that flow's in the Blood.

65. Only the Hope holds the Hand to the Success.

66. A Happy life contains the long Hard-work behind it.

67. An Animal can teaches the much more batter then the Human.

68. Heart, Soul, and Body together combine to make's the Perfect Person.

69. Advantage and Disadvantage is always walking with each other as the Light and Shadow.

70. Dare the Fault, to make it correct.

71. Efforts are the Pillar of the Success.

72. Courage becomes the Ladder to the Success.

73. Charming Works are much more difficult than the Labor works.

74. Success is never be known's the Language, it's only known's the Hard Work.

75. A Performance makes the Ten-times better then the before.

76. Angriness is the First evil towards the Success.

77. No one can understand you, much better than your -self.

78. No one can solve your problem; you have to understand it on your-Self.

79. Never be taking any step without the Permission of the Mind and Heart.

80. Happiness increases the Possibility of Success.

81. Very one have the ride to See the Dreams, but who works hard to complete it, they are the True Viewers.

82. Nature, Looks and Personality ever attracts the Target towards the Person.

83. M 84. Formula to be the Successful - Will + Hard Work = Success.

10. DESTINATION

01. Destination is the Goal, that's set-up to Achieve.

02. Every Destination ever conations the some Difficulty to reach it.

03. Destination is only the Desire, to be fulfilled.

04. Destination is the Rough over view to achieve the Target.

05. Desire make's the Destination.

06. Target is ever achieved by the Walk on the correct Destination.

07. Nothing is Pre-decided or in the God's hand.

08. Destination is ever set up the Goal, to achieve it.

09. Destination is gifted as the Mindset of the Human to achieve the Single vision.

10. Goals are ever set for achieving the something, but the Problems are ever set for ignoring it.

11. Destination is the Seed, which grow-up by the Hard working or caring it to have the Fruits.

12. Difficulty is not mean to Turn-up the Face from it.

13. Limitations are only that, that's you can set-up by your Self.

14. Every beautiful forest conations the some Hungry Fox waiting for food.

15. More attractive things are always lead to the Lose.

16. Every beautiful thing snuffer's a lot of efforts to have the Beauty, Like – Diamond.

17. Strugglers are always waiting for the Chance to perform its best.

18. Never be leaving the Hand of Positiveness to have the Success.

19. How to Catch a Dream? Is doesn't matter. Matter is that, you want to catch the Dream or not?

20. You have to orientate your way towards the Destination.

21. Dreams are the Seed of the Destinations.

22. Perfection does not exist in the World.

23. Hard work is only the Position that you can't enjoy.

24. Desire takes the long Time to grow up as the Reality.

25. Nonsense is also a great stage to have the great Experiences.

26. Every End denotes the Beginning of the New.

27. Problems are the Beat to awake you from the Sleep.

28. Hard-work is ever leads to the Perfectness.

29. Forget the Weaknesses, ever remains only the Strength that you have.

30. If you can't help the others, then never be disturbing the others.

31. Think Positive and Act Positive to Have the positive.

32. Never be stand in the Flock, create the Personality that other's are stand in the Flock for you.

33. Only a seed can creates the big Tree.

34. Time management can makes the Human as the Smart Business Man.

35. Hunan make it's on status.

36. When something is not in your destiny then it never be yours, how much you can put the Efforts on it.

37. Difficulty is not mean to Turn-up the Face from it.

38. Limitations are only that, that's you can set-up by your Self.

39. Every beautiful forest contains the some Hunger Fox waiting for food.

40. More attractive things are always lead to the Lose.

41. Every beautiful thing snuffer's a lot of efforts to have the Beauty. Like a Diamond.

42. Strugglers are always waiting for the Chance to perform its best.

43. Never be leaving the Hand of Positiveness to have the Success.

44. How to Catch a Dream? Is doesn't matter. Matter is that, you want to catch the Dream or not?

45. You have to orientate your way towards the Destination.

46. Dreams are the Seed of the Destinations.

47. Perfection does not exist in the World.

48. Miracle is only the Combination of
Believe + Efforts = Miracle.

49. Be the Power, Be the Hero, Be the Master.

Miracles of the Life

** Emotions and Feelings can understand without a Word.*

** Lover's - Will to Love, will to Chase, will to be Happy, will to never be forget, will to never be left the Hand Life Long.*

** Love is the Seed, that ever grew-up from the depth of the Heart.*

** Happiness is the Sweet Fruits of the Life.*

** Dare the Challenges to dare the Dreams.*

** Talent is ever known by the Performance.*

** Bounding is only the Pre-Decided target, that's set-up by your Self.*

** Great Challenges always brings the great Opportunities.*

** Attraction creates the Love.*

** Love ever birth in the Depth of the Heart.*

** Love is the Game of Loving Hearts, Heartless people can't effort it.*

** Sometimes Silence is more painful than the Noise.*

** A longer relation-ship is always held on the Truth.*

** Blessings and Feelings are work very quickly, but it's too effetely.*

** An attachment of the Hearts birth's the wireless Connectivity between the Persons.*

** Power is never be gifted, Power is ever be generate by the Long Meditation.*

** Raising the Power means the rising of the Opportunities.*

** Experiences are the Supporters of the Life, to create the Support in* *the Life.*

** Potential is the Power to be the Successful Person.*

** Difficulties introduce the true Caring or Faithful Persons of the Life.*

** Style is the makeover of learning's in the Behavior or Nature of a Person.*

** Every-one is expert in giving the Advice, but no one known's the Reality.*

** Different Styles makes the Human different from others.*

** Human taste can also change with the Time.*

** Past is the Story, Present is the Realty and Future is the Dream.*

** Nonsense is also a great stage to have the great Experiences.*

** Every End denotes the Beginning of the New.*

** Problems are the Beat to awake you from the Sleep.*

** A Laugh can delete all the Negative set up's in the Mind.*

** Every Relation-ship creates it's on Chemistry.*

** Thoughts are the Seed of the Mind.*

** Sleeping is the best Treatment to overcome the Stress.*

** Relations are not based on the Blood sometimes connectivity of the Heart is more than the Blood Relations.*

** Fun is the moment when the Happiness and the Human can interface with each other.*

** Every beautiful thing is not as beautiful as it looks like.*

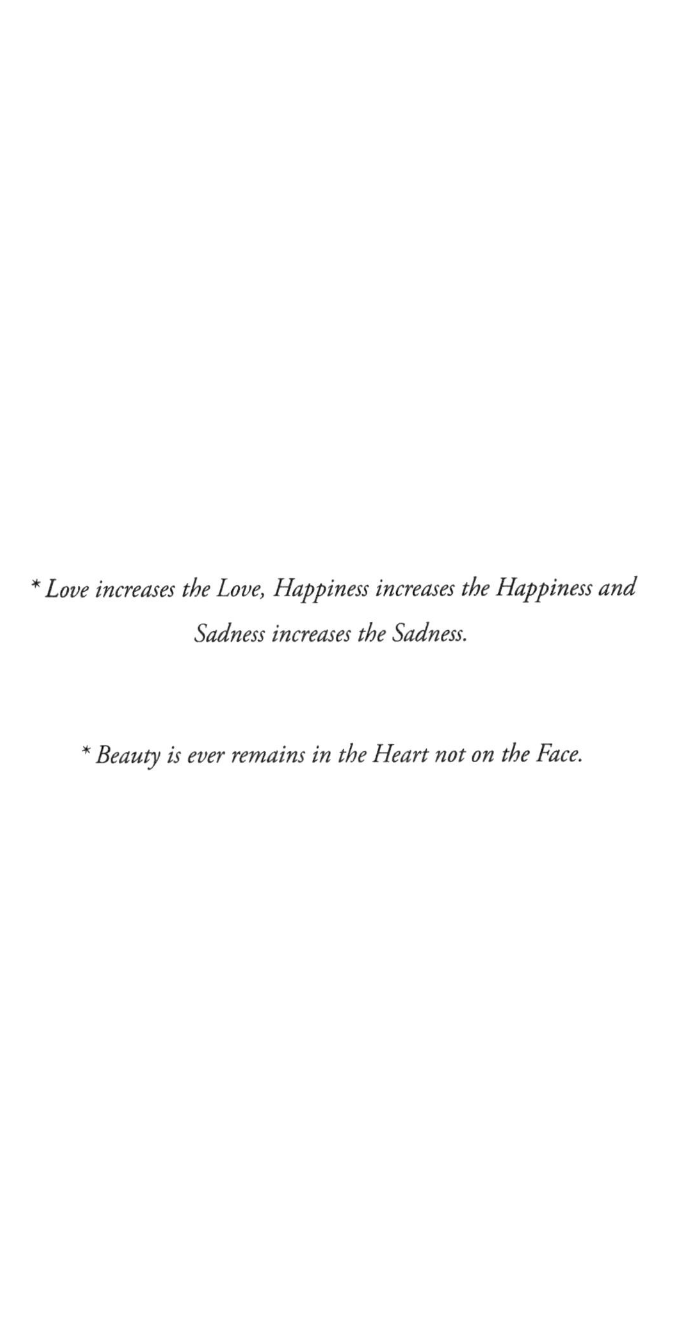

** Love increases the Love, Happiness increases the Happiness and Sadness increases the Sadness.*

** Beauty is ever remains in the Heart not on the Face.*

Printed by Libri Plureos GmbH in Hamburg,
Germany